LOUISIANA'S PLANTATION HOMES
The Grace and Grandeur

Text and Illustrations by Joseph Arrigo
Photographs by Dick Dietrich

Voyageur Press

LOUISIANA'S PLANTATION HOMES
The Grace and Grandeur

Voyageur Press

To all who love plantation lore and especially to those who own, maintain, operate, and manage the plantation homes. An extra thanks to Mrs. Helen Crozat of Houmas House, Mrs. Debra Purifoy of Tezcuco, and Mrs. Phyllis Barraco of Destrehan for their help through the years.

Text and illustrations copyright © 1991 by Joseph Arrigo
Photographs copyright © 1991 by Dick Dietrich

Printed in Hong Kong

96 97 98 99 00 8 7 6 5 4

Library of Congress Cataloging-in-Publication Data

Arrigo, Joseph A., 1930–
   Louisiana's plantation homes; the grace and grandeur / Joseph Arrigo : photography by Dick Dietrich.
      p. cm.
   Includes bibliographical references.
   ISBN 0-89658-122-5
   1. Plantations—Louisiana. 2. Plantations—Louisiana—Pictorial works. 3. Architecture, Domestic—Louisiana.
4. Architecture, Domestic—Louisiana—Pictorial works. 5. Louisiana—Description and travel—1981-—Views.
6. Louisiana—History, Local. I. Dietrich, Dick. 1927-. II. Title.
F370.A77   1990   90-44419
976.3–dc20   CIP

Published by Voyageur Press, Inc.
P.O. Box 338
123 North Second Street
Stillwater, MN 55082 U.S.A.
In Minn 612–430–2210
Toll-free 800–888–9653

Voyageur Press books are also available at discounts for quantities for educational, fundraising, premium, or sales-promotion use. For details contact the marketing manager. Please write or call for our free catalog of publications.

Contents

CONTINUED

Preface

Of the several thousand plantations that existed in Louisiana before the Civil War, a thousand or so still remain. This book is a celebration of those homes that still exist, a tribute to the original builders and to those who have restored them. The criterion used to select the plantation homes featured in this book was simple: The houses, at least at the time of this writing, were open to the public.

Though this book is not specifically intended as a guide, I hope it encourages readers to visit these interesting and beautiful historic treasures. With that thought in mind, Dick Dietrich found beautiful, fresh angles from which to capture these homes on film, and my own vignettes highlight special characteristics of each home.

All those who envisioned, designed, and built these beautiful structures, as well as those who renovate, preserve, and maintain them, deserve our thanks.

—Joseph A. Arrigo

DESTREHAN MANOR – GALLERY

Introduction

In the 1700s and 1800s, southern planters were among the wealthiest people in America. The planters in Louisiana, as in the rest of the South, built magnificent private structures in which to live, entertain, and exhibit their affluence.

Though many of those imposing buildings no longer exist, the ones that do are marvelous examples of Greek Revival and other neoclassical styles of architecture. Of course, these buildings were designed to do more than reflect classic architecture: They were functional homes designed to be comfortable. Land, climate, and location usually determine design and materials used for dwellings, and these factors obviously influenced the building of Louisiana's plantation homes. The Louisiana climate—hot, humid, almost tropical for three-fourths of the year—dictated special design features. The planters built thick walls for insulation, high ceilings and large doors and windows for air circulation, and wide galleries for shade. Often they raised the homes high off the ground to protect from flooding and to catch the breezes. At times the brief Louisiana winters were bitter, and designers strategically located the fireplaces to ensure the warmth and comfort of the planter and his family. They also cleverly designed some of the homes' heating systems to burn gas manufactured on the site; Nottoway's fireplaces featured this functional and unique amenity.

The century that passed between the building of the oldest and newest houses is reflected in their changing styles of architecture. Elaborate eighteenth-century houses such as Magnolia Mound, Parlange, and Destrehan (later remodeled) are West Indian in style, featuring raised, airy designs with wide galleries encircling the buildings. At about the same time, a simpler, less pretentious design evolved, called Louisiana Cottage. Mount Hope, Acadian House, and the Edward Douglas White House are fine examples of this style.

As more and larger fortunes were made, the planters' tastes grew more sophisticated. This created a competition among the planters to build the most elaborate dwelling. Greek Revival became the style of the day, and white pillars became the fashion. This style of architecture predominated in the last twenty-five or thirty years of pre-Civil War home building. Georgian, Italianate, and Victorian touches were added, but basically Greek Revival remained dominant until the war ended the era.

Because of the long distances between plantations, planters' homes served many purposes that city dwellings did not. Because there were no paved highways nor even railroads, travel was slow and hotels and inns were mostly in the city. The planters' guests, even those from only a few miles away, often stayed overnight. Thus architects designed the homes to accommodate guests, and the guests were treated royally during their visits. From this arose the tradition of Southern hospitality.

In their homes, the planters entertained friends and relatives, practiced religion (churches were scarce), and engaged in politics (most plantation owners were involved directly or indirectly in politics). The planters' children were born at home, and sometimes members of the families asked to be buried on the plantation grounds.

But above all else, the planters of Louisiana oversaw the production of labor-intensive crops. Among the early money-producing crops was indigo. The product of this plant is a blue dye, which was also used in ancient India and Egypt. Growing indigo eventually was abandoned because of its production difficulties and its harmful effects on the health of the slaves. Later studies have shown it to be a carcinogen.

Sugar and cotton evolved as the most successful crops. Cotton was much easier to plant and care for than indigo; even the youngest of slaves participated in its harvest. Sugar created much wealth very quickly. Both crops required a large work force, making the plantations dependent upon the slavery system. Sugarcane was, and still is, the predominant crop in the southern delta section of Louisiana, while cotton flourished in the hilly north central sections. Some of the state's plantations produced both crops.

The planters' ostentatious way of life is shown by the grand homes featured in this book. This way of life, dependent upon slavery, triggered many of the underlying controversies of the American Civil War. Louisiana and other southern plantation owners had developed the region and controlled the area's economic and political power. Slavery was the key to the labor-intensive crops that produced the wealth. Thus, emancipation was a real threat to the very source of the planters' wealth and power. Or so they thought.

It seems to us now that the southern leaders, had they just a little foresight, should have known that their cause was doomed from the start, if only for the obvious reasons of the North's overwhelming manpower and industrial ability to produce the tools of war. However, as in most wars, tightly held emotions overrule reason. The final result of the South's loss was indeed the end of the feudal plantation system that enabled the beautiful homes in this book to be built.

* * *

As you contemplate the vignettes, photographs, and stories, here are some points to consider about the distinctiveness of the area's architecture, people, and traditions:

❧ South Louisiana has more wetlands than Holland has. The state's largest city, New Orleans, is mostly below sea level. The "land" of southern Louisiana is actually of mud and silt brought down by the Mississippi River and its tributaries from twenty-three states. Hence the very earth on which southern Louisiana planters made their fortunes, and for which they fought a war, came from states as far away as North and South Dakota, Montana, and Wyoming.

❧ Many of the homes were actually built by slaves whose ranks included skilled craftsmen and artisans.

❧ Though most of the bricks used in the construction were made of native clay, very few slave cabins were brick. The primary reason: Reportedly, many slaves believed that brick harbored evil spirits and caused sickness.

❧ Because of the constant threat of floods, the main living area was often on the second story.

❧ Louisiana's early rulers were the Spanish and the French. The influence of these two countries' laws and language is obvious in the construction of many of these houses. The Spanish rulers taxed all enclosed areas, so most of the homes built during their reign had outdoor stairways, no closets, and no storage rooms. What was called a porch elsewhere was a portico, veranda, or gallery in Louisiana. What is a county in the other forty-nine states is a parish in Louisiana, a holdover from Spanish and French religious heritage.

❧ Each home has its own place in history, its own unique story. Most of the homes in this book were affected by the Civil War in one way or another. Many were destroyed; some were fired upon but survived; some were used as troop headquarters or hospitals; and two, Houmas House and Chretien Point, were saved by their owners' quick thinking and ingenuity. Several are said to be visited by ghosts having their own legends.

LOUISIANA

Natchitoches
○ ● MELROSE

Mississippi River

Alexandria
○ ● KENT HOUSE

LOYD'S HALL ○

THE COTTAGE
GREENWOOD ○ ○ ROSEDOWN
HIGHLAND ○ ○ CATALPA
THE MYRTLES ○ ○ OAKLEY
○ ○ ASPHODEL

MAGNOLIA RIDGE
○
CHRETIEN POINT

PARLANGE ○
Baton Rouge
MAGNOLIA MOUND ○ ● MOUNT HOPE ○
○ ASHLAND
Lafayette ● NOTTOWAY ○ ○ BOCAGE ○ SAN FRANCISCO
ACADIAN HOUSE ○ THE HERMITAGE ○ New Orleans
HOUMAS HOUSE ● BEAUREGARD HOUSE
SHADOWS-ON-THE-TECHE ○ TEZCUCO ○ DESTREHAN MANOR
ARLINGTON ○ OAK ALLEY
OAKLAWN MANOR ○ MADEWOOD ○
FRANCES ○
EDWARD DOUGLASS WHITE MEMORIAL
○
SOUTHDOWN

GULF OF MEXICO

Acadian House

Restored and furnished with authentic Acadian fixtures, Acadian House now serves as a museum and is the focal point of an 180-acre state park called The Longfellow–Evangeline Commemorative Area. The park and museum are located along Bayou Teche near St. Martinville, Louisiana.

This typical Louisiana Creole raised cottage was built in about 1765 by Chevalier M. D'Auterive on the property he received from a Spanish land grant. Records show that the house was sold in 1778 to the widow of Pierre De La Houssaye, the former commandant of the Spanish provincial militia at St. Martinville. (St. Martinville was once known as the Attakapas Post, so named for the Native American Indians from that area.)

Several other notable families owned the plantation through the years. Then, Louisiana acquired the property in 1931. The state park, including Acadian House and several other structures, depicts life in an early Acadian community.

The most fascinating story about Acadian House is similar to the legend told in Henry Wadsworth Longfellow's poem "Evangeline." The poem tells the tragic tale of the Nova Scotia French, who, refusing to swear allegiance to the British Crown, were forced into exile, starting life all over in settlements along the East Coast of America and in South Louisiana. The somber legend of Emmeline Labiche also tells of a modest Acadian girl. Though separated from her true love, Gabriel, at the time of the exile, she never stopped loving or searching for him. She finally caught sight of her beloved under a magnificent oak tree along Bayou Teche, only to discover that Gabriel had been unfaithful to his promise to her and married another. This tragic turn of events caused her to lose her mind, and she died a short time later of a broken heart. The oak tree has since been known as Evangeline Oak.

A different version of the story's end had the sad, disillusioned girl become a nun because of her despair, tending to her former betrothed as he lay dying from a fatal disease.

Another magnificent 500-year-old oak tree shades the lawn near Acadian House. It is appropriately called Gabriel Oak. The charming house was completely restored in 1976, and it is open to all who want to view its beauty and picture its legend.

Arlington

The lands of Arlington plantation extended on both sides of Bayou Teche east of Franklin Parish in St. Martin Parish. The builder, Euphrazie Carlin, acquired most of the land from his father, Honore Carlin, and purchased the rest from a relative in 1856. The house, built in the middle 1880s, is in the then-trendy Greek Revival style. The façade features a pedimented portico supported by four wooden Corinthian columns. The rear of the house, which faces the bayou, is identical in design, though in recent times the rear galleries have been enclosed in glass. Smaller wings on each side, added at a later date, were demolished in the 1965 restoration, which returned the house to its original configuration. The wooden house is painted white. Balustrades on both the upper and lower galleries are of elaborate wrought iron. The pediment is decorated with dentils matching those along the entablature and a large starburst medallion in the center.

In Arlington's interior each spacious room is adorned with a plaster medallion; each is different and all are original to the house. The ceilings are fourteen feet tall. A beautiful curved stairway rises in the right wing's hall from the lower level. Elaborate ceiling cornices, now redone in wood to match the plaster originals, are other features worth noting. Only one of the marble mantles is original to the house.

Local tradition avers that Euphrazie Carlin was a free man of color and owner of many slaves. But despite his great wealth, he was never accepted by his race-conscious neighbors who eventually brought him to ruin. Records show that he sold the property in 1867 to James Todd two years after the Civil War. No money actually changed hands at this transaction because Mr. Carlin's debt to the Todd family equaled the price of the property.

An 1880 Act of Sale shows that Todd sold Arlington to Charles P. McCan and John B. Lyon. Ownership again changed hands in 1884 when a New York bachelor bought the property. Eventually the Sully Martel family acquired Arlington and restored the house in 1904. Thirty-one years later, the Clarence Lawless family began a second partial restoration.

Senator and Mrs. Carl Bower acquired the house in 1965 and restored the house to its original plan. Some of the furniture already in the house was included in the interior redecoration. The lawn and gardens were also refurbished at that time.

Arlington has also been known as the Old Baker Place during its long history. Two other plantation homes in Louisiana are also named Arlington—one is near Washington in St. Landry Parish and the other is in East Carroll Parish; the latter served as headquarters for the victorious Federal forces in the Battle of Vicksburg.

Ashland

About ten miles up the river from Burnside, just above Darrow, Louisiana, stands Ashland, a majestic Greek Revival house. Designed by James Gallier Sr., the home was built by Duncan Ferrar Kenner for his bride, Nanine Bringier, of the aristocratic Creole Bringier family. The house is "temple-like" in its appearance—massive, square, thirty-foot-high columns surround the structure on all four sides. The columns support a hipped roof, which is all but invisible because of the huge entablature. A twenty-foot-wide gallery midway up the columns surrounds the stucco-covered brick walls. Ashland's interior plan is rather simple: Large center halls with three rooms on each side grace both levels. The most imposing interior feature is the beautiful spiral staircase, which boasts treads of cypress and balustrades of mahogany. The staircase winds gracefully from the main floor at the end of the hallway to the attic. Mantles enhance the fireplaces in the large rooms although some of the mantles are now gone. Windows in all the rooms extend to the floor and open to the gallery.

Duncan Kenner was one of the wealthiest, most prominent, and most influential men in the history of Louisiana. He was noted for not only an economically successful sugar operation and business dealings but also for his large library, hospitality, knowledge of wines, and stable of thoroughbred horses, which he raced at his own track on the plantation grounds. However, Kenner was not as lucky as a politician. He was defeated in his pursuit of a seat in the U.S. Senate by Judah P. Benjamin in 1851. He later became a delegate to the Secession convention in Montgomery, Alabama, and rose to a high rank in the Confederacy.

In 1862 Kenner escaped from his house when Union soldiers landed nearby. Though he was one of the South's largest slave holders, he made a startling suggestion to Confederate president Jefferson Davis. His idea was to free the slaves, an act that would negate the North's humanitarian appeal and, he hoped, gain the assistance of France and England. In 1865 President Davis appointed Kenner to be the Confederacy's minister plenipotentiary to Europe with powers to implement his slave-freeing policy to get help for the faltering Confederacy. Kenner managed to reach Europe, slipping through the Yankee blockade, but the effort was too late: The Confederacy had all but crumbled and the war was almost over. Kenner returned to Louisiana, eventually regained his fortune, and lived at Ashland until his death in 1887. He was seventy-four at his death; his wife lived to be eighty-eight.

Ashland, named by Duncan Kenner after the Kentucky home of one of his personal heroes, Henry Clay, was eventually sold to John B. Reuss. Reuss renamed the estate Belle Helene for his daughter, Helene Hayward. For a number of years the house rested empty, but a restoration was begun by the descendants of the Hayward family in 1946; the restoration continues today. The unrestored sections of the first floor give visitors a view of architectural aspects not usually visible in completely restored homes.

Asphodel

In 1833 Benjamin Kendrich built this smallish Greek Revival on a knoll overlooking Carr's Creek near the town of Jackson, Louisiana, in East Feliciana Parish. It stands in a beautiful setting well back from the road. *Asphodel* is from Greek and is used poetically to mean daffodil, a flower that grows abundantly in the area.

Kendrich unfortunately died the year the finishing touches were completed on the house. Because he had no sons, the property passed on to his only daughter, who had married David J. Fluker. The cotton and cane plantation prospered, allowing the Flukers to pour much of their wealth into their home and its surroundings. They had twelve children, traveled extensively, entertained lavishly, and were fashionably involved in politics.

The house is built of locally molded bricks covered with stucco made from the fine sand of a nearby stream. Six white Doric columns support a gabled roof, which features two dormer windows. On each side, joining just behind the exterior side chimneys, matching set-back wings look like miniatures of the center portion.

During the Civil War, Yankee soldiers involved in the nearby Battle of Port Hudson raided the plantation in search of food and supplies. They set fire to the house; fortunately the flames died quickly after they left and the structure was saved.

The family lived in poverty after the war, as did most plantation owners. One by one the children matured, married, and left to survive on their own as best they could. After the turn of the century the plantation was occupied by two spinster sisters, Kate and Sarah Smith, descendants of the Fluker family. They remained at Asphodel until their deaths in 1945 and 1948. Both are buried on the grounds in the family cemetery. One of Asphodel's tales says that the two sisters never left the plantation during the forty years they lived there.

Mr. and Mrs. John Fetzer purchased Asphodel in 1949 and restored the house to its original grandeur. In 1958 after Mrs. Fetzer's death, the Robert Couhigs acquired the property. They added bathrooms, a large kitchen, a gallery, and even a swimming pool. The Couhigs also moved a cabin built in 1850 to the grounds and opened it as a restaurant. More cottages and buildings were added, creating a resortlike atmosphere for overnight guests.

Several movies have been filmed at Asphodel, the most notable being "The Long Hot Summer," which starred Paul Newman, Joanne Woodward, and Orson Welles.

Beauregard House

This house stands in Chalmette National Historic Park, site of the Battle of New Orleans, and was built about two decades after the War of 1812 with England. Some historians attribute its original design to the noted New Orleans architect James Gallier Sr., and the design for later remodeling is credited to his son, James Gallier Jr. Records show that the land on which the house was built was purchased by Alexandre Baron, the Marquis de Trana, in April, 1832. Baron authorized construction of the house, originally called Bueno Retiro or "Sweet Seclusion." For years the house has been called Beauregard House after its last private occupant, Judge Rene Beauregard, son of the famous Confederate soldier, General P. G. T. Beauregard.

Judge Beauregard and his family lived in the house from 1880 until 1904. After that it remained empty and dilapidated. When the National Park Service acquired the home in 1947, Beauregard was nearly destroyed. Sam Wilson, dean of local architects, took responsibility for restoration. The result of his expertise and efforts is viewed by thousands who visit the park and house each year. Relics, mementos, and a diorama of the great Battle of New Orleans are on display in a nearby building.

In recent years Beauregard House has been restored by the National Park Service to its original beauty of detail and color. Lining both the front and the rear, eight Doric columns support wide galleries. The attractive hipped roof has dormer windows perched on all four sides.

The simple floor plan, only one room deep, opens each of the six rooms (three on both levels) to both façade and rear galleries. An indoor staircase on the downriver side connects the two floors. The galleries facing the river are connected by an outdoor stairway. Wings on each end of the house, added after the original construction, were not restored.

One of the most interesting construction details of the house is the two fireplace chimneys that blend into one in the attic by means of an arch. The central chimney then projects from the roof just below the roof ridge, and only one chimney appears outside.

The apricot-colored plaster walls, the white columns, the balustrades and roof entablature, the blue-green shutters, and the purple-gray slate roof are set against a backdrop of moss-draped oaks, and the soft colors and details all blend to make Beauregard pleasing and picturesque.

Bocage

Bocage translates to Shady Retreat. The plantation home was built in 1801 by Marius Pons Bringier as a wedding gift to his daughter Françoise and her husband Cristophe Colomb, an alleged descendant of the famous explorer. Bringier, head of the wealthy and powerful Bringier family, owned several plantations along the Mississippi River in South Louisiana.

Françoise, at the time of her wedding, was only fourteen years old; her husband Cristophe was thirty-one. Cristophe was quite a remarkable character: He was involved in the French Revolution and escaped from his native country to flee the guillotine. His departure reportedly led him to his uncle's island plantation in Santo Domingo, where a slave uprising forced him to flee again—this time to Philadelphia and then on to French Louisiana.

Cristophe and Françoise's relationship was very unusual for the time, but it was harmonious. Fanny, as she was popularly known, had inherited the Bringier aptitude for business, and ran the plantation. Cristophe's talents, however, were in the arts: He was an accomplished singer, musician, poet, and dancer. The usual roles were thus reversed in this marriage. Fanny directed the work in the cane fields and sugar mills, while her husband wrote poetry and entertained at their social gatherings. He even had a fancy boat built for himself, with a silken canopy and friezing on the sails. His slaves rowed the boat along the bayous and waterways, taking Cristophe to relatives and friends.

The two-story house itself is almost square, constructed of wood on the upper level and brick on the lower level. Its front gallery is supported by six large square pillars and a pair of smallish pillars at the center, forming a novel façade. A high entablature with Empire details hides the roof and most of the chimneys. After a fire in the late 1830s Bocage was extensively remodeled, emphasizing Greek Revival and Empire detailing. Bocage and many of its counterparts fell to decay and abandon after the Civil War. It was rescued by Drs. E. G. and Anita Crozat Kohlsdorf, who restored the home and gardens to their former glory. Their restoration included furnishing the house with elegant antiques. Mr. and Mrs. Richard Genre are the present owners; Mrs. Genre is the niece of the late Anita Crozat Kohlsdorf.

For years the house has been open to plantation tours by appointment. It is located about two miles north of Burnside along the east bank of the Mississippi.

Catalpa

This charming Victorian cottage was built by William J. Fort in 1885 to replace the original house, which was destroyed by fire. William Fort came to the Feliciana country from the Carolinas with skilled servants to erect the first Catalpa. The Forts raised both cotton and sugar. They were successful planters and shared their good fortune with family and friends, almost constantly giving parties and providing entertainment at their home.

The house was elegantly furnished, but the true beauty of this estate was its grounds. A parklike atmosphere was created using exotic plants, flowers, and fruit trees that were developed and nurtured in a large hot house. The extensive garden included a pool, a deer park, shady sitting areas, peacocks, pigeons, and other exotic animals.

Invasion by Union troops during the Civil War destroyed the original house and its grounds. Almost everything edible was foraged by the hungry army. Fort died during this time, but his widow, Sally, held on to the property; she determinedly rebuilt the house almost immediately after it burned. Fortunately much of the furnishings were saved and are still in use today. Other fine pieces were acquired from Rosedown Plantation when it sold in 1956. Sally Bowman Fort was the daughter of Sarah Turnbull of neighboring Rosedown, and James Pirrie Bowman, of nearby Oakley.

Two notable features of this estate are the unusual elliptical alley of moss-draped oaks, a beautiful corridor to the house, and the steadfast ownership (the property remained in the same family since first built). I visited Catalpa in 1985. It was then occupied by Mamie Fort Thompson and Sadie Fort, both great-granddaughters of William J. Fort.

The thirty-acre gardens have been returned to their parklike beauty, with plantings of hydrangeas, azaleas, camellias, and a large variety of trees and plants natural to the area. Though this restructure is not strictly antebellum, Catalpa is one of the most charming of the Louisiana planters' homes open to visitors. It is about three miles out of St. Francisville and is open daily for tours.

Chretien Point

In 1776 a Spanish land grant awarded Pierre Declouet a rise of ground about eight miles from what is now the city of Opelousas. Hippolyte Chretien, one of three brothers from France, purchased the property in about 1800 to raise cotton, the popular crop of the area.

Stories mention the friendship that Hippolyte had with the brothers Jean and Pierre Lafitte, who used Chretien Point to conceal and move some of their smuggled cargo—and slaves. These tales are credible because Chretien accumulated hundreds of slaves to work his ever-increasing cotton-producing acreage in a seemingly short time.

In 1812 during the Battle of New Orleans, Hippolyte Chretien and some of his neighboring planters joined the pirates Lafitte and General Andrew Jackson in this fight, which defeated the British. One of the gentlemen that fought with Chretien was a man known only as Señor Neda. Neda's daughter Felicite married Hippolyte Chretien II and became one of Louisiana's first "liberated" women. Behaving very unconventionally for her time, Felicite was active in the management of plantation business, smoked cigarettes, and even was adept at card gambling. Felicite increased the plantation holdings by whatever methods she could. She acquired much property because of her proficiency at cards as well as her dealings with New Orleans bankers and businessmen, almost unheard-of activities for a woman at that time. Her courage and self-sufficiency were more than helpful because her husband and one of her two sons died from yellow fever shortly after the house was completed. She unearthed his money, which was buried on the grounds, after convincing Hippolyte's faithful servant, Pajo, to reveal its hidden location.

This remarkable lady also possessed physical courage: It seems she herself thwarted a robbery attempt by shooting a thief in the head and frightening off his accomplices by confronting them with the possibility of a similar fate.

During the Civil War, a battle fought on the plantation grounds was led by Federal general Nathaniel Banks and Confederate general Alfred Mouton. Hippolyte Chretien III, though sick and feeble, saved the house by giving a secret Masonic sign that was honored by General Banks, a fellow Mason. Though the house was spared, the rest of the plantation buildings were destroyed by Yankee forces.

Hippolyte III inherited the plantation and lived at Chretien Point with his wife, Celestine Cantrell, and their son Jules. Jules was a multitalented young man, and unfortunately the family was more interested in the creation and appreciation of the arts and not in the practical science of management. After several crop failures the family attempted rice production, which also failed. The property was eventually lost to the mortgage holders. Jules became a traveling salesman of kitchen utensils.

The house was restored to its original magnificence in the late 1970s. The six-brick Tuscan pillars at front are based on square foundations that anchor the wide, wooden, balustraded gallery; the pillars rise two stories to the eaves of the hipped roof. Round-headed French doors and windows are features in each room. Chretien Point's great room is graced with unique mantles of verde-antique Italian marble with Ionic capitals and shelves of black onyx. Ceiling medallions are elaborately carved. Exterior walls are eighteen inches thick and the house measures sixty-three feet wide by forty-seven feet deep.

Sadly, the original furnishings were destroyed by fire after they were moved to a small hotel, which was operated by one of the Chretien heirs. The present owners, the Cornay family, have again beautifully furnished the house and graciously opened it to plantation tours.

CHRETIEN POINT – SITTING ROOM

CHRETIEN POINT — DINING ROOM

19

The Cottage

In 1811 Judge Thomas Butler purchased the tract of land about nine miles north of St. Francisville where The Cottage stands. The original land grant was awarded by the Spanish to John Allen and Patrick Holland in 1795. The basic house was expanded by the Butler family several times and is now a complex of several buildings. Judge Butler was the son of Colonel Thomas Butler who, with his four brothers, fought with distinction in the Revolutionary War under General George Washington. Colonel Butler was later court martialed for refusing an army order to cut his queue (gentleman's braid) at the back of his neck. He died at Ormond Plantation in Destrehan, Louisiana, of yellow fever, still wearing his beloved queue.

The main structure is a rambling, two-story home made of cypress with extremely wide galleries in the front and rear. The roof, extending over the galleries, is supported by evenly spaced colonettes. The rear wing, a later addition, was so well planned it seems part of the original building and has seven columns rising from its gallery. The galleries' balusters are of cypress. An unusually large number of doors and windows open to the galleries on both the rear wing and the main house.

The Cottage's furnishings reflect the early owner's affluence. *Faux–bois* was used extensively to alter the cypress woodwork so that it appeared as other fine woods.

Imported English wallpaper with 14K gold leaf was used in the main parlor, and is still in the home. Draperies on the windows were (and still are) "puddled" on the floor, another decorating tradition showing affluence.

The outer buildings that still survive comprise the kitchen (now an antique and gift shop), the stable (still housing the Butlers' carriage), the barn, and two of the slave cabins. A small family cemetery still remains.

The property was sold to Mr. and Mrs. J. E. Brown of Chicago in 1961. Frequent guests at The Cottage, they became so enchanted they purchased it from the Butler descendants. Mr. Brown, while employed as an engineer-executive for the Zenith Electronic Corporation, was noted for his inventions that helped to develop the color television tube.

Two of The Cottage's more illustrious guests have been General Andrew Jackson, and Grand Duke Alexis of Russia, who traveled disguised as Lieutenant Romanoff to avoid any special reverence in "democratic America." One of the property's slave cabins was used as Cicely Tyson's quarters in the award-winning television series "The Autobiography of Miss Jane Pittman."

The Cottage's twenty rooms are open to the public and overnight accommodations are available in its several antique-furnished bedrooms.

THE COTTAGE – BEDROOM

22

THE COTTAGE – LIVING ROOM

23

Destrehan

Destrehan Manor overlooks the east bank of the Mississippi River several miles above New Orleans. In a contract, translated from French and still on file at the local courthouse, it is written that in 1787 "Robert Antoine Robin de Longy and Charles [Pacquet], free mulatto, have agreed . . . that the said Charles, carpenter, woodworker and mason by his trade, obligates himself to construct . . . a home of sixty feet in length by thirty-five feet in width . . . for the sums and price mentioned hereafter . . . one brute Negro, a cow and her calf . . . fifty quarts of rice in chaff, fifty quarts of corn in husks and one hundred piastres [dollars]." Pacquet took three years to complete the house. DeLongy died in 1792, enjoying his house but a short time. His son-in-law, Jean Noel Destrehan, acquired the house in 1802. He was a wealthy Creole who, while serving in the Louisiana Legislature, helped write the state constitution.

The plantation first raised indigo, corn, and rice. But soon they converted to growing sugarcane, a much more lucrative crop after Etienne deBore discovered an inexpensive method of granulating sugar in 1795. During Destrehan's lifetime the plantation grew extensively.

Like many planters along the Mississippi, Destrehan was as interested in having a large family as he was in producing sugar. The solid brick garçonnieres, somewhat attached on both sides of the main house, were additions to accommodate the increasing family. These two new units, though slightly asymmetrical in size, conformed so well with the original West Indies–style architecture, they seemed part of the structure.

In 1823 Stephen Henderson, a wealthy Scotsman, took Destrehan Plantation over. He married Lelia Destrehan; her death preceded her husband's though she was only half his age. Henderson died in 1838, leaving a most complicated will. Because the will was contested by his surviving relatives, most of its provisions were set aside by the Louisiana Supreme Court. Henderson had directed that upon his death his slaves be emancipated, given an acre of land, a mule and a cow, or, if they chose, given passage to Liberia. The litigation over this and other then-controversial philanthropic provisions in the will continued for years, and most of the estate went for legal fees.

In 1839 Judge Pierre A. Rost, another son-in-law of Jean Destrehan, acquired Destrehan Manor. Rost began an extensive renovation, altering the house's West Indies appearance to conform with the then-popular Greek Revival style. Great white pillars were formed by covering the earlier wooden colonettes with brick and plaster. The original *bousillage entre poteaux* (Spanish moss and sand between posts) walls were lathed over, plastered, and scored to resemble granite stones.

One of Destrehan's outstanding architectural features is its high-peaked West Indies–style roof. Three smallish dormer windows and two asymmetrical chimneys jut out from the roof. The original heart-of-cypress, hand-hewn beams are visible throughout the house. Also in the house is a large marble bathtub said to have been a gift from Emperor Napoleon I to Jean Noel Destrehan.

Many noted guests were entertained at the manor house during the years the Destrehans and their descendants occupied the property. Two of the most famous were the Duc d'Orleans, who became king of France, and the renowned pirate-hero Jean Lafitte, whose ghost appears during stormy nights pointing to where he hid some of his treasure.

Union forces seized the house during the Civil War and turned the property into a Freedman's Bureau colony, housing hundreds of newly freed slaves. The property was returned to the Rost family through presidential intercession in 1866, and remained in the family until 1910.

Since 1914, Destrehan has been the property of various oil refining companies that still utilize some of the acreage. In 1972 the manor house, devastated by neglect, vandalism, and the elements, was donated to the River Road Historical Society. This dedicated, nonprofit group began an immediate restoration of the manor house and several acres of picturesque grounds. Today, Destrehan Manor House is open daily to the public. All proceeds from admissions, annual festivals, and profits from the charming antique and gift shop are dedicated to Destrehan's continuing restoration.

DESTREHAN MANOR – BEDROOM

DESTREHAN MANOR – LIVING ROOM

27

Frances

Frances was built in 1820 by Louis Demaret, a native of Dunkerque, France. He purchased the property from Marc Navarro, who had acquired the land by a grant from the Spanish government. The Demaret family was one of the first to settle in the area. But not until more than a half century later did the home receive the name Frances. In 1879, Louis Kramer gained ownership and named the home after his daughter.

The attractive, simple house stands along the bank of Bayou Teche near Franklin, Louisiana. It is a two-storied raised cottage built of brick on the first floor and of red cypress on the second floor. Four square brick columns support the second-floor front gallery, which is bordered by a wooden balustrade. On both the first and second floors, rhythmically spaced windows with doorways between each window open to the galleries. The windows' glass panes and shutters are original to the house. Four square wooden colonettes rising from the second-floor gallery support the roof, and two outer chimneys project upward on both sides of the house. Attractive carved fireplace mantles in the house are also noteworthy.

Nineteen-sixty-three saw the beginning of a complete restoration. The house opened in 1965 as an antique and gift shop but has ceased to operate as such since the late 1980s. The many beautiful antique silver, china, and furniture pieces made shopping at Frances almost like a visit to a museum. The rear gallery has been enclosed in glass; it overlooks magnificent oaks leading down to the banks of the bayou. The front of the property features a curved drive and a charming landscape. Several outbuildings and a large green cistern have been moved to the grounds from nearby plantations. The house is shown only by appointment.

Greenwood

Greenwood, the largest plantation house in the Felicianas, is a restructure. William Ruffin Barrow built the original in 1830 on the 12,000-acre sugar and cotton plantation he purchased from Oliver Pollack, who had acquired the land by grant from the Spanish government. The Barrow family, originally from England, had emigrated first to the Carolinas before settling in the Feliciana country. They prospered in Louisiana, probably building more large plantation homes than any other single family.

Greenwood, with the exception of the twenty-eight brick columns, was built of lath and plaster. The Doric columns, thirty feet tall, rise from an elevated porch to hold a large roof entablature unusually decorated with triglyphs and other designs. Within the four corner columns, roof drains feed below-ground brick cisterns. A belvedere straddles the roof. Originally about forty outbuildings and 100 slave cabins were on the grounds.

Judah P. Benjamin, the noted Confederate statesman and a close friend of Barrow, advised his friend to sell the property because of the approaching Civil War. At a great loss Barrow sold the plantation intact to the Reed family. Federal troops did overrun Greenwood, destroying most of the outbuildings, but sparing the main house for use as a hospital. The Reed family retained the property, living there and maintaining the home until 1906.

Greenwood was then sold to Mr. and Mrs. Frank S. Percy, who restored it and eventually opened it to the public.

In 1960 tragedy struck: A huge fire destroyed the house, leaving only the twenty-eight columns standing. Greenwood remained a ruin until 1968 when the charred remains and 300 acres were purchased by Baton Rouge attorney Walton J. Barnes and his son Richard.

The two men then began a most ambitious project: a reconstruction of the house as it originally was. Since no plans existed, the Barneses duplicated the structure by researching hundreds of old photographs and by interviewing those who had visited and lived at Greenwood.

Greenwood once again lives! Its twenty-eight majestic white columns are reflected in the original pool, dug to provide the clay for the columns' bricks. The interior once again boasts an impressive central hall that is seventy feet long, with a curved wooden stairway at one end. Its furnishings reflect the style of the 1830s. Silver doorknobs and other hardware, ruined in the fire, have been remade.

The house has been used as a locale for several movies. The most notable to date is "North and South," a television miniseries about a family during the Civil War.

Greenwood is open to the public daily for tours.

The Hermitage

The prominent French Louisiana family of Emmanuel Marius Pons Bringier practiced an interesting tradition: They gave a plantation, complete with manor house, as a wedding present to each child. The Hermitage was one of those presents.

Michel Doradou Bringier, one of Emmanuel Bringier's sons, married Louise Elizabeth Aglae duBourg de Sainte–Colombe in 1812. She was fourteen years old when she married, was born in Jamaica, and was educated in Baltimore by nuns. She was also the niece of the Bishop of New Orleans, Louis William Valentin duBourg.

The War of 1812 took Michel Doradou away from the plantation. He nobly served with General Andrew Jackson and returned in 1815, at about the time construction was being completed on his manor house. He named it The Hermitage after General Jackson's Tennessee home, to honor his much-admired commander. To his French Louisiana relatives and neighbors, the home, of course, immediately became "l'Hermitage."

Elizabeth outlived Doradou by thirty years; he died in 1847. She had grown from a child bride to a self-confident plantation mistress, managing the business successfully through the Civil War times. The house was fired upon by Federal troops but survived intact, being hit by only one cannonball.

After the war, Louis Bringier, one of Michel and Elizabeth's sons who had served as a Confederate army colonel, took over the plantation's operation. Against all odds and with the help of some of the former slaves who now worked as free persons, he successfully produced profitable sugarcane.

Eventually Duncan Kenner of Ashland, who had married into the Bringier family, acquired the property. In the 1880s it was acquired by the Maginnis family, then by the Duplessis family, then by the LaSalle family, and in 1959 by Dr. and Mrs. Robert C. Judice of New Orleans. The Judices have completed a faithful and beautiful restoration.

Designed with splendid simplicity, The Hermitage is built of thick "brick-between-post" construction and smoothed over with plaster. Massive Doric columns and wide galleries sweep around the house. Two dormer windows are perched on a typical hipped roof. The interior is beautifully furnished with decor and furniture in the pre–Civil War style.

Evidence suggests that the house had been remodeled in 1849, probably by the noted New Orleans architect James Gallier Sr. The encircling galleries originally had brick pillows below and wooden colonettes above, typical of the time of its construction. They were replaced by the well-proportioned pillars as seen today.

The Hermitage is open by appointment for group tours.

Highland

Highland is the first home built by the Barrow family, one of the wealthiest and largest plantation families in Louisiana. Highland was constructed sometime between 1799 and 1805 by Mrs. Olivia Ruffin Barrow, a widow from the Carolinas who envisioned the Felicianas as a land of opportunity for her sons and daughters. The Spanish rulers of the Felicianas welcomed these and other industrious English families to help develop this cotton-growing country. However, the Spanish rule was overthrown in the early 1800s. The Felicianas then became an independent republic for several months until being absorbed by the United States.

The house was constructed by slave labor, some quite skilled, with materials found on the plantation grounds. Only the window blinds were "factory-made"—cut of local cypress lumber shipped to a Cincinnati mill. Poplar was used for wainscoting and doorways. All other construction is of cypress, including floors two inches thick.

Highland was designed more in the Carolina Federal style than in the then-common Louisiana Planter style. The front gallery features six squarish cypress pillars with horizontal cross-braces at approximately midlevel. There is no second floor gallery. In 1832 Bennett Barrow planted a grove of 150 oaks, now reaching splendid maturity.

The years just before the Civil War were the most prosperous for this farm. In the 1850s Highland consisted of more than 4,300 acres, cultivating both sugar and cotton. The plantation had its own sugar mill, hospital, and even its own race track.

Bennett Barrow changed the name of the plantation to Highland after a variety of cotton he developed. It had originally been called Locust Ridge. Descendants of the Barrows still reside at Highland. Though the acreage is smaller than it was during its glory days, it is still under cultivation, mostly as pastureland for cattle grazing. The house was renovated in 1960 and is beautifully maintained and open to the public by appointment.

Houmas House

This beautiful, white-pillared mansion sits on a strip of land along the Mississippi once inhabited by the Houmas Indians. It is an ideal model of a Louisiana plantation manor house—a symmetrical house in a symmetrical setting among 200-year-old moss-draped oaks and huge magnolias.

John Smith Preston, son-in-law of the Revolutionary War general Wade Hampton, built Houmas House. General Hampton made his fortune planting cotton in South Carolina, and when assigned by the military to Louisiana, Hampton saw an opportunity to increase that fortune with Louisiana sugarcane. He became one of the first non-Creoles to do so. When again reassigned, this time away from Louisiana, his daughter and her husband, John Preston, came from South Carolina to supervise the Louisiana holdings. In 1840 the Prestons began constructing their magnificent Greek Revival mansion in front of an original four-room structure, which in later years was attached to the newer building.

The house is two and one-half stories high, with a glass-enclosed belvedere at its roof peak. Fourteen Doric columns enclose three sides of the home; the columns also support galleries around three sides. Dormer windows project from the hipped roof on all sides. Two hexagonal brick garçonnieres, or bachelors' quarters, each with a first-level sitting room and a second-level bedroom, are on either side of the main house. Inside a masterfully crafted circular stairway, seemingly unsupported, rises to the third-floor attic.

In 1857 the Prestons sold Houmas House and 10,000 acres to John Burnside, an Irish emigrant who had made a fortune in New Orleans as a merchant. Burnside increased the acreage twofold, building four sugar mills to process the crops he grew on his 20,000 acres. A true "sugar-prince," Burnside lived life to the fullest, lavishly entertaining his many guests at Houmas House.

Houmas House suffered less from the Civil War than other river plantations did. When the feared Yankee general Ben Butler approached Houmas House to take it as a headquarters, he was defiantly backed off by Burnside, still a British citizen, who threatened international complications if the general entered his house as a military leader or as a representative of the United States.

John Burnside remained a bachelor until his death in 1881. He left the house and acreage to Oliver Bierne, a member of the family who had helped the young Irishman get his start. William Miles, husband of one of the Bierne daughters, acquired the property and increased its productivity to an even higher level. After Miles's death in 1899, the property was slowly divided and sold away, the grand house left to deteriorate.

Houmas House and the remaining acreage was purchased in 1940 by Dr. George B. Crozat, the first Creole to own the property in more than 100 years. He immediately began a restoration of house and gardens as seen today. Many of the antique, museum-quality furnishings came from his family home in New Orleans.

This home has been featured in many periodicals; it has also been the setting for numerous Hollywood and television movies, the most noteworthy being "Hush, Hush, Sweet Charlotte," starring Bette Davis. Houmas House is still owned, maintained, and operated by gra-cious members of the Crozat family. It is open daily for tours and is a must for antebellum plantation buffs.

HOUMAS HOUSE – SPIRAL STAIRCASE

HOUMAS HOUSE – GARCONNIER

HOUMAS HOUSE – LIVING ROOM

40

HOUMAS HOUSE – KITCHEN

41

Kent House

Pierre Baillo, originally from Natchitoches, Louisiana, migrated to the Bayou Rapides area in about 1790. He built the central section of Kent House a short time later in the French Colonial style—two large, very plain rooms opening to front and rear galleries. The rear gallery features wooden louvres to allow in light and air, but also to give protection from rain. This architectural detail can also be found at Oakley, which is near St. Francisville. This main part of Kent House is constructed of *boussilage*—mud, moss, and animal hair between cypress beams.

The two rectangular wings that flank the front gallery were added in the 1840s by Robert Hynson, the second owner. The house probably acquired its name during this period. The oldest part of the house features a central chimney, which services the fireplaces in each of the large rooms. Each side wing has a fireplace on its exterior wall.

The wings and the original central rooms and galleries are raised high above the ground on brick piers. An unverified story tells about these tall piers: When Pierre Baillo began work on the foundations for Kent House, he started the slaves on construction of the brick piers and then left to go to New Orleans to acquire furnishings, assuming he would return before the work on the piers would be completed. He was delayed, however, and when he did return he found that the slaves had continued to build the piers higher and higher.

Inside this restored, simple house are seven rooms decorated with excellent examples of Federal, Sheraton, and Empire furniture. Also featured are some charming pieces made by native Louisiana cabinetmakers. The floors are made of cypress as are the beams, gallery columns, and balustrades.

Kent House, an excellent example of rural Louisiana architecture, is said to be the oldest standing structure of its kind in Louisiana. It stands as the focal point of a four-acre, parklike site with out-buildings, grounds, and herb garden all reflecting a lifestyle of the early nineteenth century. Cooking demonstrations featuring early cuisine are given in the "working" kitchen. At the front of the house, a white wooden picket fence surrounds flower gardens with patterned beds.

The property is located in Alexandria, Louisiana, on Bayou Rapides Road, and is open daily to the public.

44

Loyd's Hall

Such little archival information is available about this property that tracing its history has been enigmatic. Some historians claim the house was built in 1810, some say it was built in 1816 and remodeled in 1830. The author of *Rapides Parish*, a history of the parish in which Loyd's Hall stands, states that the house was built a short time before the Civil War.

It is known, however, that the house was built by a wayward member of the Lloyd's of London family. It seems this Lloyd was granted property in the central Louisiana parish with the stipulations that he emigrate there, never return to England, and change his name. He complied with the last demand by eliminating the second *l* from his name and therefore the name of his new house.

Loyd's Hall stands majestically by Bayou Boeuf, near the old "Texas Trail." It is an eclectic blend of classic architecture: The two-and-a-half-story central portion is Georgian in style. It is constructed of slave-made brick and features chimneys that are built into the exterior walls and form a U shape on the top of the roof. The Greek Revival front gallery has six white, slender, squarish cypress columns resting on stouter, squarish brick pillars. The gallery railings are of cast iron. Much of the extensive detailing exhibits Victorian influence. Another unique architectural feature of the exterior is the galleries' roof design: both galleries' roofs and the main roof slope to allow the draining of water where they join.

Inside the house are twenty-by-twenty-foot rooms with sixteen-foot ceilings and elaborately detailed cornice moldings and ceiling medallions. The doors are of cypress, the floors of heart-of-pine, and the stairway railings are of maple. Twenty-eight large, shuttered windows are symmetrically situated in the eighteen-inch-thick walls. Somewhat recently, Mrs. Virginia Fitzgerald began a restoration of this noble residence, rescuing Loyd's Hall from the humiliating fate of ruin. Dr. and Mrs. Frank Fitzgerald have continued the preservation and restoration and have graciously opened the house to the public.

Loyd's Hall has not one but two resident ghosts: One is a Yankee soldier who, badly injured during one of the nearby Civil War battles, died in one of the slave cabins while being secretly nursed by Sally Bonton, a plantation slave. His body was hidden and not discovered until years later when the skeleton was accidently found. Supposedly his ghost appears regularly in the house. The other ghost that appears occasionally is that of a Confederate soldier who was hanged on the Loyd's Hall grounds. He appears at night, sometimes playing the violin. When I visited Loyd's Hall several years ago, Mrs. Fitzgerald told of the ghostly appearances, stating that her daughters have seen the apparitions many times and that the ghosts are quite friendly.

Madewood

Along Bayou Lafourche, at Napoleon-ville, stands Madewood, a magnificent white mansion designed by the noted New Orleans architect Henry Howard. Colonel Thomas Pugh, scion of the prolific, wealthy, and powerful Pugh family, began construction in 1840 after a four-year effort of felling, planking, and hand-hewing pine and cypress from the plantation grounds into "made-wood." Construction of this large home took four years; its stucco-covered brick walls range from eighteen to twenty inches thick, and more than 60,000 slave-made bricks were used. Its foundation was designed of solid slablike stylobate in the Greek temple fashion. The house's majestic façade features six huge, fluted, Ionic columns, a wide pediment, and diamond-shaped balusters surrounding the gallery. The outline of the two small wings on each side is proportional to the lines of the center structure.

Unfortunately Colonel Pugh died of yellow fever in 1848, just prior to Madewood's completion. His widow, Eliza Foley Pugh, a descendant of one of the few Anglo-Saxon settlers in the area, completed the house, though not exactly as it was originally designed: She made one of the wings into a 24-by-48-foot ballroom.

The interior of Madewood is as magnificent as the ex-terior. Dramatic features are the very high ceilings with ornate medallions and chandeliers; cornices with elaborate dentils; window frames; cornices and doors finished in *faux-bois* (cypress painted to resemble oak); marble fireplaces; an unsupported, heavily carved stairway; and elaborately carved Corinthian columns as well as smaller, fluted, Ionic columns. The antique furnishings, though not original to the house, impressively match the structure's majestic architectural details.

The Pugh family survived the ravages of the Civil War intact and their descendants remained at Madewood until 1916. The property was then acquired by Mr. and Mrs. Robert L. Baker, and then sold to Mr. Bronier Thibault in 1946. Madewood is now owned by the Harold K. Marshall family, who took possession of the mansion in 1964.

The Marshall family has restored the house to its present, beautiful condition. The Marshalls have added a large collection of furniture and art objects from other plantations, area antique shops, auctions, their own family, and even from the New Orleans Museum of Art. Madewood is open to the public for tours and for overnight accommodations in the sumptuous bedrooms.

Magnolia Mound

The glacial outwash from the Pleistocene Epoch carved out the Mississippi River valley and created a series of ridges in the Baton Rouge area. Magnolia Mound stands atop one of these ridges, which is along Nicholson Drive, near the campus of Louisiana State University.

Magnolia Mound was built in 1791 to serve as a residence for the 1,000-acre plantation. The first crops grown were tobacco and indigo. John Joyce, a Mobile, Alabama, merchant, bought the plantation from James Hillin, who acquired the land by grant from Spain in 1786. Joyce died in 1798; his widow later married a neighbor, Armand Duplantier, a prominent Baton Rouge citizen, and *aide-de-camp* to the Marquis de Lafayette. About this time the plantation converted from growing tobacco and indigo to cotton.

Magnolia Mound is often identified with Prince Charles Louis Napoleon Achille Murat, a nephew of Napoleon I and the son of the king of Naples who reigned from 1808 to 1815. Prince Murat occupied the house, seemingly as a guest of the Duplantiers because no record exists of any purchase or rental transaction, while the Duplantiers lived at another of their properties. The prince, according to local legend, was a man of eccentric habits. He supposedly liked eating delicacies made from alligator tails, owls, rattlesnakes, and other oddities. He was also known for his dislike of bathing, for not paying his debts, and for continually chewing tobacco. Prince Murat eventually emigrated to Florida, married a grand-niece of George Washington, and became an alderman and the town postmaster. His other accomplishments were literary: He wrote several books about his American travels, which became very popular in Europe. Prince Murat died in 1847.

The plantation was growing sugarcane when George Hall acquired it in 1849. Hall and his wife lived in Europe during the Civil War, leaving the estate in the hands of an overseer. When Baton Rouge fell in 1862, Federal troops occupied the house and grounds. The Halls sold the property to Helen McCullen in 1869. Ownership changed hands again in 1883. Later, Louis Bariller bought out his partners who had been running the plantation and was the last to operate Magnolia Mound as a family-run cotton and sugar plantation.

Robert A. Hart, a successful Baton Rouge businessman, took over the property in 1904. He subdivided and developed the plantation as residential plots because the urbanization of the city made lots more valuable than farmland. Descendants of the Hart family occupied the house until the early 1960s.

Magnolia Mound, when first built, had a direct view of the Mississippi River. The house, originally built as three rooms, was expanded by Mrs. Duplantier by adding a dining room and two service rooms. Today, the interior is furnished in the Federal period. Wooden balustrades adorn an eighty-foot-wide front gallery. Square wooden columns support a hipped roof with two dormer windows. A central chimney serves back-to-back fireplaces.

The house, scheduled for demolition to make way for a large apartment building, fortunately was saved by the Foundation for Historical Louisiana after a stalwart and bitter legal battle. The foundation has since beautifully preserved this interesting house and opened it to the public.

Magnolia Ridge

Located near Washington, Louisiana, this classic mansion was originally known as the Old Prescott House and later as Oakland Plantation. It was built in the 1830s by William Marschall Prescott and has been inhabited by several generations of the Prescott family. William Prescott died in 1854 and is buried on the grounds in an old family cemetery with many other family members.

One of the most notable in the family was Captain Lewis Prescott. He achieved fame in the Confederate Second Louisiana Cavalry with his command, Company A, the last organized Confederate military group to surrender to the Federal army (June 5, 1865). During the Civil War, Magnolia Ridge was a headquarters for the Confederate army and later for Federal forces.

The house is built on a rise surrounded by huge magnolias and oaks. It overlooks Bayou Cotableu just inside the Washington town limits. Originally called Church Landing during the steamboat era, Washington was the second largest such port in Louisiana. Cotton, the major crop, was loaded here to be shipped eventually all over the world.

The structure is two and one-half stories high, built of brick and painted white. Six Doric columns, supporting a second-story gallery and a gabled roof, line the front of the house. Center doorways with transoms and sidelights are aesthetically placed on both floors. Two windows, with jalousies on each side of the central doors, are also identically spaced on each floor. No dormer windows interrupt the sloping roof. The two chimneys, one at each end of the house, are built within the walls.

Mr. and Mrs. George Wallace of Baton Rouge purchased Magnolia Ridge in 1939. Mrs. Wallace was a descendant of William Marschall Prescott, the original builder. The Wallaces restored the house as a residence, somewhat modifying the floor plan by adding bathrooms and a modern kitchen. The second floor and the attic have bedrooms and bathrooms, and all levels have a central hallway. In 1948 the property was again sold, this time to the Valery Mayers family.

Magnolia Ridge is a focal point in the prominent and historical town of Washington, Louisiana. The gardens are open for daily tours.

Melrose

Melrose Plantation, an interesting complex of structures, is near the city of Natchitoches, the oldest settlement in the Louisiana Purchase. Melrose stands along a bend in the Cane River. Augustin Metoyer, a free man of color, built Melrose in 1833. The main house was constructed by free mulatto workmen directed by Louis Metoyer, son of Augustin, who was given this property along with a large number of slaves.

Melrose was originally called Yucca, presumably because of the abundance of that spearlike Spanish plant on the grounds. The original residence is now known as Yucca House and stands behind the main house in almost its original condition. Another building has puzzled historians and architects alike. Called African House, it is a story and a half tall, brick, with a mushroomlike, overhanging roof, similar in appearance to West African structures. Its precise function has never been explained but is now used as a museum.

The lower level of the main house is made of brick, including the pillars extending to the floor of the wide front gallery. The second level is constructed of mud, moss, and cypress. The house is only one room deep with doors and windows strategically placed on both levels to allow for cross-ventilation. Though the octagonal towers on each end were added much later, they blend beautifully with the original architecture. A single chimney and dormer windows extend from the hipped roof.

Cammie Henry came to live at Melrose in 1899. "Miss Cammie" was the real force behind the preservation and restoration of the plantation as it is seen today. An authority on Louisiana lore and history, Miss Cammie filled her collection of scrap books with material about the state starting just after the death of her husband John Henry; it is one of the most complete collections of information about Louisiana history ever made. Miss Cammie made Melrose a mecca for writers and artists. To anyone seriously interested in painting, drawing, or writing about Louisiana, she made her collection completely accessible in a relaxed and hospitable atmosphere. Many literary and artistic figures of international repute worked at Melrose, including the now-famous primitive artist Clementine Hunter, who created thousands of paintings here, most of which depict life on this plantation. Another of Miss Cammie's exceptional achievements is the garden she landscaped. Flowers, shrubs, trees, and many exotic plants now proliferate from her plantings. Several variations of native Louisiana iris she developed have been named in her honor.

Melrose, though not as pretentious as some of its counterparts, radiates a true feel for living in an atmosphere of happiness and comfort. It is open daily to the public.

Mount Hope

Just outside of Baton Rouge, Joseph Sharp, a German native, built a raised cottage with an unusual roofline and called it Mount Hope. The plantation's property had been acquired from the Spanish government in 1786. Most area historians surmise that the house was constructed just before the 1790s, but the exact date is undocumented.

Mount Hope fronts Highland Road in a picturesque area of Baton Rouge called the Dutch Highlands. This is actually the first region along the Mississippi River delta that was naturally high enough to be protected from the occasional flooding that occurred before the days of artificial river levees. During the Civil War, Confederate troops camped on the grounds under the same beautiful oaks still standing today.

Except for the roofline, the architectural style follows the usual Louisiana Cottage style of the early 1800s. A wide gallery, with wooden colonettes and balustrades, encircles most of the structure. Windows and doors are placed to allow maximum air circulation. Ceilings are twelve and one-half feet high.

Mount Hope saw many owners through the years until 1917. The family that purchased it then kept it until 1970, when Arlin K. Dease acquired the plantation and began a complete restoration. Dease later restored Nottoway and The Myrtles as well. Mount Hope has remained in the Dease family and is now owned by Mr. and Mrs. Jack Dease, who open the house daily to visitors and offer bed and breakfast accommodations. Mount Hope is also a gracious setting for weddings, parties, and banquets. The interior is beautifully furnished with Federal, Sheraton, and Empire pieces.

MOUNT HOPE – FRONT GROUNDS

56

MOUNT HOPE—LIVING ROOM

The Myrtles

Just off U.S. Highway 61, north of St. Francisville, stands The Myrtles. The home is nestled in a large grove of live oaks and is surrounded by mimosas and azaleas. But it is christened The Myrtles for the lovely myrtle trees on the grounds.

The original 650-acre property was a land grant awarded to General David Bradford, a veteran of the 1794 Whiskey Rebellion. Judge Clark Woodruff, son-in-law of General Bradford, constructed The Myrtles in 1830 on the site of an earlier residence.

The story-and-a-half wooden house is extremely wide; its gallery, elaborately embellished by New Orleans—style cast iron in a grape-cluster pattern, extends across the entire 120-foot façade.

Eight pairs of French doors open all along the gallery, and the main entrance's door frame features a modified Greek key design. Two room-size dormer windows, set between three smaller ones, project from the slanted roof.

Details inside The Myrtles are exquisite. They include elaborate ceiling medallions and friezes and fretwork decorating all sides of the double parlors. The mantles are made of Carrara marble and *faux-marbe*. The door-knobs, most unusual, are mercury enclosed in glass and were designed never to need polishing. Leaded glass windows, *faux-bois* wood-work, and Baccarat crystal chandeliers are other outstanding interior features. Suprisingly, some of the rooms contain closets, an unusually extravagant feature of the time since they were taxed as separate rooms.

Recently, Arlin K. Dease, restorer of Mount Hope and Nottoway, renovated The Myrtles with Mr. and Mrs. Robert Ward of Baton Rouge. The owners have begun to offer overnight accommodations, sometimes hosting "theme" weekends in which murder mysteries relating to the house are played out by the guests. And the mysteries have a real-life tinge. Several murders are supposed to have taken place in the house. One involved a gentleman killed during a gambling argument. His ghost is allegedly one of several residing at The Myrtles. According to another legend, the ghost of a little old lady, always wearing a bonnet, drifts from bedroom to bedroom in search of someone she never finds. Other stories tell of the appearance of a ghost of an infant who died there and yet another who never quite makes it up the main stairway.

The house is open to the public.

THE MYRTLES—SITTING ROOM

THE MYRTLES – DINING ROOM

61

Nottoway

Nottoway, the largest of the existing plantation homes, was built in 1857 near Bayou Goula on the west bank of the Mississippi. Nottoway has sixty-five rooms and almost 65,000 square feet!

In 1841, John Hampton Randolph, a descendant of a famous Virginia family, left Woodville, Mississippi, to build this huge dwelling. The empire of plantations he created eventually amounted to more than 7,000 sugarcane-producing acres.

Randolph and his wife had eleven children, eight girls and three boys, making them known for their large family as well as the vast sugarcane operation. A large family required a house of suitable size, and the affluent planter began work on Nottoway by soliciting designs from the prominent architects of the day.

The winning proposal came from the distinguished New Orleans architect Henry Howard, who designed Madewood in Napoleonville and many other notable structures. Randolph liked this plan, a magnificent Italianate, primarily because it was quite different from the Greek Revival mansions Randolph's fellow planters were building.

Nottoway has a large stucco-covered brick basement supporting two main stories. Twenty-one tall, squarish columns support iron-railed galleries on the first and second level. A tall entablature almost completely hides the hipped roof. Two grand, curved stairways rise from the front entrance. Nottoway boasts of some imposing interior furnishings: 200 large windows, some with curved glass; large stately doors with hand-painted door knobs and sterling silver hardware; and the large, first-level, sinuous ballroom finished completely in white, including mantles, chandeliers, Corinthian columns, and even the floor! The beautiful room served its purpose well: Seven of Randolph's eight daughters married, their weddings occurring in the famous white ballroom. Other notable features in Nottoway were running water and indoor bathrooms on each floor! The fireplaces burned gas manufactured on the plantation site.

The house and family survived the Civil War, but after the death of Mr. Randolph in 1887, Mrs. Randolph sold Nottoway to Dr. W. G. Owen. An Owen descendant recently sold the house to Arlin K. Dease, the same gentleman who restored Mount Hope and The Myrtles. Dease immediately began to restore the home and opened it to the public for the first time in 1981, offering overnight accommodations. Dease has since sold the house to the present owners who continue to operate Nottoway as a house and museum with bed and breakfast accommodations and catering services for almost any event.

NOTTOWAY – GRAND BALLROOM

NOTTOWAY – MUSIC ROOM

65

NOTTOWAY — SUN ROOM

NOTTOWAY – BEDROOM

NOTTOWAY – DINING ROOM

68

NOTTOWAY – BEDROOM

69

Oak Alley

In the late 1600s or early 1700s, an unknown French settler transplanted many young evergreen oaks from the riverbank to a double row near his small cabin. At that time, this was a wilderness above the settlement of New Orleans. Eighty feet apart, the twenty-eight oaks are now in full-grown splendor and form a stagelike cavernous aisle, the most imposing "oak alley" in the Mississippi valley.

Jacques Telesphore Roman, brother of a governor of Louisiana, built his mansion in 1836 at the end of this magnificent line of oaks on the site of the original planter's cabin. He chose this exact site to showcase his sumptuous residence, but the oaks themselves, in their own natural splendor, dominated the setting. They still do.

Roman originally named the house Bon Sejour, "Good Rest," the name of his wife's family property in France. The towering oaks, however, have caused the estate to be popularly known as Oak Alley.

American architect George Swainey designed this splendid house in the Greek Revival style so prevalent at the time. Jacques Roman seemed to follow his numerical hunches. Because twenty-eight oaks lined the aisle, twenty-eight columns surrounded the house, and even twenty-eight slave cabins were built. Oval, fanlighted doorways, with wide, side sunlights, are at each end of the hallways that run through the house on both floors.

The hipped roof has a balustraded belvedere at its peak. On each side of the roof, one chimney and three dormer windows project symmetrically. The plastered exterior walls and columns were, and still are, painted pale pink.

Though Oak Alley suffered no damage from any Civil War action, the Romans' finances did. The family was forced to leave the plantation after the war. During the Southern reconstruction period it was occupied by the Sobral family, the Haydel family, and several other families.

As the economic fortunes of the area dwindled, the house began to deteriorate gradually, until it was abandoned and left to the ravages of nature. About the time of the First World War the Jefferson Hardin family acquired the estate and operated the property as a farm. Fortunately they repaired the roof and structure enough to stop the rain's destruction. Even more fortunate for Louisiana, Mr. and Mrs. Andrew Stewart bought the house and acreage in 1925. They immediately began a complete "adaptive" restoration, added necessary conveniences, moved in, and graciously opened their showplace home to the general public.

Since Josephine Stewart's death Oak Alley has been operated by a nonprofit foundation. We hope the home will always remain open to visitors as a symbol of Louisiana's architecturally glorious plantation homes.

OAK ALLEY — DINING ROOM

OAK ALLEY – BEDROOM

Oaklawn Manor

Oaklawn Manor, one of the most impressive antebellum plantation homes in Louisiana, is located along Bayou Teche in the Irish Bend section between Franklin and Jenerette, Louisiana.

Entrance to the plantation is through two old iron gates opening to a long winding drive that ambles through what is reportedly the largest grove of live oaks in the country. The magnificent white mansion revealed at the drive's end was originally built in 1837.

Alexander Porter, originally from Ireland and later from Nashville, was a family friend of General Andrew Jackson. It was Jackson who urged his industrious young friend to settle in Louisiana. In 1809, acceding to General Jackson's suggestion, Porter settled along Bayou Teche and began acquiring property in order to farm sugar. The affable young planter quickly made friends with his neighbors, became involved in politics, and was elected to the legislature where he helped write the state constitution. Porter's political career eventually included twelve years as an associate justice of the Louisiana Supreme Court and service as a U.S. Senator. He also founded the Whig Party in Louisiana. Porter's marriage to Evilina Baker in 1815 lasted just four years, because tragically his young wife and one of their two daughters died by 1819.

After retiring from the Senate, Porter began to seriously develop his estate. The oak trees, some growing since the time of Columbus, were pruned, and the manor house was constructed. Judge Porter lived at Oaklawn Manor until his death in 1844. When his remaining daughter died shortly after, the estate was left to his brother James. James died in 1849; only James's wife remained to run the plantation through the bad times of the Civil War. She sold the property just after the war but retained the right to reside there, which she did until her death in 1881.

The plantation changed hands several more times and slowly deteriorated. Fortunately Captain Clyde Barbour rescued the home in 1924. Barbour, a steamboat captain, had admired the house for years as he piloted his steamboat along the bayou.

The captain's restoration was halted by a huge fire in February of 1926, destroying the house's interior; fortunately, the thick brick walls and sturdy pillars remained intact. The resolute captain rebuilt the manor house with materials and furnishings accumulated in New Orleans and from all over the world. Squares of Italian marble from the old St. Charles Hotel in New Orleans, itself a victim of fire, replaced the original cypress floors. The Barbours aimed for an extravagant restructure: Belgian marble on some of the mantles; a stairway of Italian Carrara marble; hand-blown Venetian chandeliers; and even a wine cellar and a swimming pool. They also transplanted more than 100 mature oak trees to the huge grove.

Captain Barbour died in 1931, but his wife lived on at the plantation for another thirty years. In the early 1950s her daughter and son-in-law, Mr. and Mrs. Thomas Holmes, came to Oaklawn to live with her.

In 1963 Mr. and Mrs. George B. Thompson bought the property and began another renovation, adding air conditioning and many new and elaborate furnishings. In 1985 the estate became the property of the Murphy J. Fosters, who have added even more furnishings to the house: A collection of Audubons, Selbys, and Don Gomez wood carvings are splendidly displayed.

The 15,000-square-foot manor house features six Tuscan columns in front, and oversized, fanlighted, arched doorways at each end of the first- and second-floor central hallways. The third floor, built as a large ballroom for entertaining, was a favorite room during the Judge Porter days.

Much of the woodwork in the house is original; fortunately it was saved from the 1926 fire. Silver doorknobs and keyhole escutcheons ornament the large doors. Another notable detail is the crosslike motif found on each door, supposedly designed to protect the plantation from evil spirits.

Oaklawn Manor has its own ghost story: The apparition, according to local legend, is that of a young woman and a girl who periodically prowl around the outside of the manor house. The plantation was used in the movie "The Drowning Pool," starring Paul Newman. An aviary built by the Warner Brothers studio remains on the grounds. Oaklawn Manor is open to the public daily for a fee.

O A K L A W N   M A N O R – C O U R T Y A R D

OAKLAWN MANOR — ENTRANCE HALL

77

Oakley

About twenty-five miles north of Baton Rouge, near the town of St. Francisville, stands Oakley, a large two-story frame house built over a brick basement. James Pirrie, a prosperous Scotsman, began building Oakley in 1808 on land inherited by his wife, Lucie. She was the widow of Ruffin Gray, recipient of the property by land grant in 1770.

Oakley's design is rather simple, antedating the Greek Revival style used by plantation home builders in later years. A centered, wide stairway leads to the front of the lower gallery. Wooden louvered slats cover the upper gallery and part of the lower gallery, uniquely allowing in light and air while giving protection from the elements. A restored formal garden on the left side of the house creates a winsome setting with plantings of roses, trimmed hedges, and crape myrtles all shadowed by moss-draped oaks.

Oakley's interior is one and one-half rooms deep and two rooms wide with no inside hallways. (The half-room was actually a small sleeping room for servants.) A narrow, enclosed stairway at the rear was a later addition. The Colonial and early nineteenth-century furnishings reflect the period that John James Audubon lived at Oakley while employed as a tutor for the Pirrie's daughter, Eliza. Mrs. Pirrie recruited him and his assistant, artist Joseph Mason, in New Orleans for sixty dollars a month plus room and Board to teach Elizabeth drawing, dancing, French, and etiquette. The arrangement allowed Audubon half of his time to be on his own and do as he pleased. Fortunately for nature lovers, Audubon became fascinated by the lush vegetation and wildlife and chose to draw and paint thirty-two of the birds in his masterwork *The Birds of America*.

The house was occupied by descendants of the Pirrie family until 1944. Fortunately deterioration was halted in 1947 when the state of Louisiana acquired the property from the remaining members of the Mathern family, who were related by marriage to the original Pirrie family. A complete restoration of the house and grounds created a park of more than 100 acres, which is open daily to the public. Nature trails around the house recreate the atmosphere Audubon found so inspiring. An annual pilgrimage to Oakley and other plantations in the area honors Audubon and celebrates his accomplishments.

Parlange

One of the most charming houses of earlier Louisiana vintage is Parlange, built in the early 1750s by a French nobleman, Marquis Vincent de Ternant. The property, granted to him by the French Crown, lies along False River, a cutoff section of the Mississippi that became a deep, still lake after the outlets to the river were sealed. Indigo was the first crop of the plantation, but sugarcane soon became the successful crop, as at most of the other South Louisiana farms.

After the marquis died in 1757, the plantation was managed by his son Claude. Claude married Dorothee LeGros, a widow about whom very little is known. Claude and Dorothee were married about eight years. After her death, Claude married his ward, an orphan named Virginie Trahan. Virginie and Claude had four children. When she traveled back to Paris with him, in spite of her humble beginnings she became as sophisticated as the continental society of which they were a part. The manufactured furnishings sent back to their Louisiana home attest to her acquired regal taste. Claude Ternant died in 1842. After a time Virginie returned to Paris, eventually marrying Charles Parlange, a French military officer. Oddly, the property derives its name from this man, the second husband of the second wife of Claude Ternant, the second owner.

Of Claude's and Virginie's four children, three died at a young age and a fourth married and eventually left to live in France. Her only son, Charles (from Virginie's second marriage), was with her when Federal troops arrived at the plantation during the Civil War. Forewarned of their imminent arrival, she had the servants hide the silver and valuables, which they later recovered. A story about Parlange recounts that a large amount of money remains buried on the grounds to this day.

Virginie's hospitality to the invading troops saved the plantation from destruction. She served the finest wine and food to the Union officers and even set out loaves of bread and dishes of hot food for the troops in the yard. The Yankee general Nathaniel Banks slept in one of the guest rooms for several nights. Confederate general Richard Taylor is also said to have been an overnight guest here. After the war, Parlange fell on hard times, as did its counterparts all over the South. By sheer determination and hard work, Virginie and her son kept the plantation from the ever-present creditors. Charles even became an attorney, then a state senator, then lieutenant governor, then a federal judge, and finally a justice of the Supreme Court.

The house exemplifies the classic Louisiana Creole plantation home. It is built of brick on the first level and of cypress, plaster, and mud on the second. Brick columns support the balconies surrounding the house; matching cypress colonettes support the hipped roof. Windows and doors open asymmetrically to the galleries. Two octagonal brick pigeonniers stand near the house on each side in the tradition of northern France. Inside Parlange, cypress ceilings, carved wood chandeliers, medallions, beautifully crafted door frames and moldings, furnishings, accoutrements, and artifacts are original to the house and family. The house is open to the public and is still lived in by descendants of the gracious Parlange family.

Rosedown

Daniel Turnbull, an Englishman and descendant of George Washington, built a gracious home near St. Francisville for his bride, Martha Barrow. The plantation property was originally a 1779 Spanish land grant to John Mills, a founder of St. Francisville.

In 1834, just after construction of the house was begun, the Turnbulls left for Europe to begin acquiring the furniture, chandeliers, tapestries, and other treasures needed to furnish their grand new residence. On their return trip the young newlyweds stopped in New York and attended a play in which one scene with a rose-covered wall so reminded the young bride of her new Louisiana home she decided to christen it Rosedown.

Although no proof exists, it is said that on that same European trip a prominent French landscape artist was engaged to design and construct formal gardens to embellish the Louisiana-Georgian classic mansion. A later theory holds that Mrs. Turnbull, an avid experimental horticulturist, designed the gardens herself. Martha kept a meticulous diary describing the gardens' progress, lending credence to this second theory.

The main structure is of cypress, painted white. Simple Doric columns support the roof across the front double galleries, which feature curved balusters, also of cypress. Georgian fanlights and sidelights of leaded glass adorn the front doors on each level.

Two stuccoed, brick, Greek Revival wings were added in the 1840s. Balusters matching those of the galleries topped these lateral additions. In 1859 the house was again enlarged by the addition of a bedroom wing at the rear.

The Turnbulls often traveled to Europe to acquire more treasures for their Louisiana Eden. They found Italian Carrara marble statuary for their ever-developing gardens—gardens which equalled or even possibly surpassed the elegance and classic beauty of the house. These statues, urns, and other garden ornaments, as well as century-and-a-half-old shrubs and trees, have been well preserved and maintained.

Daniel and Martha had one child, a daughter, Sarah, whose beauty was legendary. After being pursued by a multitude of suitors, she married James Pierre Bowman. They had ten children, and eight were girls.

The Civil War crushed Rosedown as it crushed most of the grand Louisiana plantations. Loss of a feudal system of cheap labor, high mortgages, low crop prices, and soil deterioration brought poverty to the once opulent estate. The Turnbull family showed their true bearing during these times, fighting all adversity as it arose. Even though Daniel died during the first year of the war, Martha, Sarah, Sarah's husband, and their ten children refused to relinquish the property. Together they assumed the responsibility of caring for the gardens, house, and fields, doing much of the physical work themselves. The mortgages were eventually serviced, a tribute to the determination and strength of the true southern family in true "Scarlett O'Hara" fashion.

Members of the Turnbull-Bowman family occupied Rosedown from the time of its construction until 1956, when the last of the Bowman daughters died. Mr. and Mrs. Milton Underwood of Houston, Texas, then acquired the property. They immediately began to restore the home and opened the plantation house and gardens to the public in 1964. This was a beautiful tribute to a family and the grandeur of their 1800s Louisiana plantation lifestyle.

Because of the continuity of the ownership, most of Rosedown's furnishings are original. The house and gardens are truly among America's most distinguished and beautiful showplaces.

R O S E D O W N – B E D R O O M

ROSEDOWN – MASTER BEDROOM

85

ROSEDOWN – ENTRANCE

86

ROSEDOWN — SITTING ROOM

San Francisco

The most unique house along the Mississippi River's "Plantation Parade" is San Francisco. This home is an eclectic blend of Victorian, Classic, and Gothic architectural styles; the result is a structure reminiscent of the ornate steamboats that plied the Mississippi in the 1800s.

The house is located in Reserve, Louisiana, along the river road abutting the levee that through the years has moved closer and closer to the house because of the river's changing flow.

Edmond Bozonier Marmillon finished building San Francisco in 1856; regrettably, he died a short time later. His son and heir, Valsin, gave it the name Sans Frusquin, a popular French expression meaning "my all" or "without funds"—supposedly the elaborate house consumed most of the family wealth. The name was mispronounced and eventually evolved to "San Francisco."

The three-story building includes a roof-top observatory. The first level is constructed of plastered brick, and *brisques-entre-poteaux* (brick-between-posts) makes up the other levels. Square brick pillars support the main gallery, which runs across the front and halfway down each side of the house. Matching each brick pillar on the second level are fluted wooden columns with cast-iron Corinthian capitals. The capitals reach shallow arches, which, in turn, support a narrow third-level deck; above the deck a huge entablature meets a hipped roof. Huge wooden cisterns on each side of the house provided running water to the house through pipes; although the pipes were of lead, running water was a feature notably ahead of its time.

San Francisco's interiors were designed to be as elegant and colorful as the fine salons of the riverboats Marmillon obviously admired. Painted ceiling frescoes and murals are attributed to the Italian artist Dominco Cardova. *Faux-marbe* techniques decorate the woodwork and fireplace mantles. Although never completed, the third-floor ballroom was planned to be the most elaborate feature of the house, to be lit by rainbow colors through glass panes set into lattices beneath the floor of the belvedere.

The second owners took the original furniture when they sold the plantation. An oil company eventually acquired the property and began a complete restoration in 1975. The ceiling frescoes have been faithfully restored, the *faux-marbe* and *faux-bois* features re-created, and the house has been beautifully and elaborately furnished in an 1856 style. San Francisco is open daily to visitors for a fee.

SAN FRANCISCO – BEDROOM

90

SAN FRANCISCO – SITTING ROOM

91

Shadows-on-the-Teche

A property of the National Trust for Historic Preservation since 1958, Shadows-On-The-Teche is an 1831 version of a Louisiana Greek Revival plantation house. The home's lush surroundings are reflected in its name. Magnificent moss-draped oaks, tall cypresses, flowering magnolias, bamboo groves, crape myrtles, jasmines, camelias, exotic ferns, and other flora all cast long, lazy shadows.

The architecture of The Shadows blends classical, Georgian, French-Creole, and Anglo-American influence. A wooden staircase on the gallery outside the living quarters and no central hallway are classical designs. Though the chimneys are contained in the interior walls in Creole taste, the mantels are English in style. Three dormer windows with double-hung sashes project from a gabled roof, an Anglo-American trait. Shutters, or jalousies as they are called locally, run from the ground to the roof between the two pairs of columns on either side of the façade. One set of columns camouflages the stairway. The other pair maintains balance, a classical requisite.

David Weeks, originally from Maryland, built this house on the banks of Bayou Teche in New Iberia, the heart of the Cajun country. The home was built as a town house, away from the several plantations operated by the family. David Weeks, born in Baltimore in 1786, was the son of William Weeks, a native of Bristol, England, who had acquired the plantation's property and several thousand acres in the vicinity. Like so many other plantation home builders, David died just as the house was completed. His widow, Mary Clara, lived in the town house with her three children; in true matriarchal fashion, she operated the family plantations. She remarried in 1831 to Judge John Moore, a U.S. congressman, Secessionist, and later a prominent Confederate political figure.

Mary Clara always managed her beloved "Shadows" extravagantly. She continuously bought elaborate furnishings and decorations to fulfill her aristocratic Virginia tastes. Her taste for luxury included food items as well: Though most plantations of this time produced most of the food required, she bought commercially produced staples, even refined sugar, to better serve her refined palate.

During the Civil War the house was occupied by Federal general Banks and his troops. Through this period Mary Clara remained at The Shadows, voluntarily confining herself to the attic, where she died in 1863. Her son William acquired the house at the Secession sale, and though his fortunes later declined, he deftly held on to the property, passing it on as a legacy to his two daughters. One daughter, Mary Lily, married Gilbert Hall and became the mother of Weeks Hall, the last landlord at The Shadows. After the death of his parents, Weeks purchased his aunt's share of the property and began the rebuilding of the house and gardens.

Weeks Hall was an unusually talented and colorful person. Though considered an intellectual, his formal education did not even include a high school diploma. His artistic talent however, did win him a scholarship to the Pennsylvania Academy of Arts and later additional scholarships to study art in France and England. He became an internationally known artist, art critic, lecturer, photographer, and gardening expert.

Restoration of the house was completed in the early 1920s. Hall spent the rest of his life sharing the ambience of The Shadows with noted visitors from all over the world—Cecil B. De Mille, Henry Miller, Tex Ritter, Lyle Saxon, to name a few. His famous white woodwork door, a collecting place for autographs of these famous callers, was once inadvertantly scrubbed clean by an overzealous servant. Hall, over a period of years, reinvited most of these noted visitors back to his house to resign their names to the door. It is still intact and can be viewed today at the house.

Hall remained a bachelor until his death in 1958. He appealed on national television to the National Trust for Historic Preservation, asking them to assume responsibility for maintaining the old homestead. He received notification while on his death bed that they had agreed to do so. The Shadows is now a permanent exhibit reflecting an interesting phase of Louisiana's heritage. It is open daily to the public.

SHADOWS-ON-THE-TECHE—CHILD'S BEDROOM

SHADOWS-ON-THE-TECHE – SITTING ROOM

95

Southdown

Southdown was built on part of a Spanish land grant to Jose Llano and Miguel Saturino. One of the several people who owned the property for a short time before the house was built was the noted adventurer and soldier Jim Bowie, renowned for the knife named after him and for his exploits at the Alamo.

Southdown's sugarcane played a dramatic role for the South. The first crop grown at Southdown was indigo but various factors made sugarcane more rewarding. On the fields of Southdown a heartier subspecies of sugarcane was developed. The new variety fought the blight and disease that had periodically attacked Louisiana's cane. Varieties of the new seed were then adopted by most of Louisiana's sugarcane planters.

In 1828, Stephen Minor, once governor of the Louisiana territory when Natchez was the capitol, purchased the plantation. In 1858, his son, William II, built the house with brick and cypress from the plantation grounds. Gothic Revival architecture was slightly less popular than Greek Revival at that time, but the Minors nevertheless chose the former. Instead of the familiar white columns, Minor erected a smallish, simple entrance gallery. The original house, completed in 1862, consisted of what is now Southdown's main floor, which includes the twin front turrets and the rear center turret. The house's walls are one foot thick. Southdown was named after a variety of sheep the Minor family imported—the Minors used the sheep to feed on the grass between the rows of sugarcane.

During an 1893 renovation, Henry C. Minor added a second story matching the first. The date is visible on a gable just above the second-floor front gallery. Southdown's twenty-plus rooms are large, with fourteen-foot ceilings and eleven-foot doorways. A stained-glass scene of sugarcane and magnolias ornaments the front door. A similar scene adorns the doorway leading from the wide hallway to the dining room. Tiny bricks compose the mantel in the great hall, an unusual design. The dining room fireplace is of slate, designed in a delicate leaf pattern.

Descendants of the Minor family occupied the house until 1923. It was then used as a residence by employees of Southdown Sugar, Inc. Then in 1976 the Terrebone Historical and Cultural Society bought the plantation and now operate Southdown as a museum. The society showcases many of the treasures and furniture of the house's heritage. Also exhibited is a collection of personal items and memorabilia of the late U.S. senator Allen Ellender. Ellender, a native of the area, was a notable and powerful national figure because of his longevity in the U.S. Senate.

In addition to the historical displays, local art shows are featured almost continuously. The house is open to the public daily for an admission fee.

Tezcuco

The reason Benjamin Tureaud named the home he built "Tezcuco" has never been determined. It might have been for the village in Mexico (he did fight in the Mexican War), or for the literal meaning of the word, "Resting Place." Benjamin, son of Augistin Tureaud and Elizabeth Bringier, of the wealthy and powerful Louisiana Bringier family, completed the house only one year before the Civil War began for his cousin-bride, Aglae Bringier. It is on the east bank of the Mississippi, about forty miles south of Baton Rouge.

The structure is built of slave-made local brick and cypress from nearby swamps. Though called a "raised cottage," the house has many refinements of a true plantation mansion. Magnificent moss-draped oaks surround the dwelling, casting flattering shadows on the entire property. Dormer windows are symmetrically placed on all four sides of the hipped roof. A broad stairway at the front gives wide access to the deep front gallery. Elaborate cast iron decorates the two smaller side galleries—reminiscent of New Orleans–style houses. Six square wooden pillars along the front gallery support the large roof entablature.

Tezcuco's interior displays a classical French influence. A central entrance hall opens to very large rooms with ceilings reaching sixteen feet. Some window frames and woodwork have their original *faux-bois* artistic finish.

In 1950, Dr. and Mrs. Potts refurbished and refurnished the house, adding an excellent collection of antique pieces by such noted furniture makers as Mallard and Seignouret. More recently, General and Mrs. O. J. Daigle acquired the property and began a second restoration in 1981. Authentic slave and sharecropper cabins moved from nearby plantations form a village, which is now used for overnight accommodations. A chapel, country store, and other interesting buildings have been built or added to the village.

In the main house the Daigles have beautifully presented their personal collection of Louisiana art, Newcomb Pottery, and fine crystal. The entire ground level "basement" now serves as a most interesting antique and gift shop.

Tezcuco is within sight of the Sunshine Bridge, so named because it was built during the administration of Governor Jimmie Davis, who wrote the song "You Are My Sunshine," reported to be one of the world's most-played songs, exceeded only by "Happy Birthday" and "White Christmas." It is open daily for tours and bed and breakfast accommodations.

Edward Douglass White Memorial

This raised cottage is an excellent example of eighteenth-century Louisiana-style architecture. It is built of hand-hewn cypress held together by wooden pegs, set on a high brick foundation, and has galleries at both the front and rear. The galleries feature wooden balustrades and square cypress colonettes supporting the dormer roof, out of which project three dormer windows. A row of slave cabins once stood behind the house.

Edward Douglass White I, one of the early settlers in Lafourche Parish, built the house in 1790. The White family, originally from Ireland, were educated nobles who first made their mark in Pennsylvania and North Carolina. White was once governor of Louisiana and then a U.S. congressman. He died in 1847 of injuries received from a steamboat explosion on the Mississippi.

Although Edward Sr.'s accomplishments were many, this house and park is a monument to Edward Jr. Edward Douglass White II was born here in 1845. He lived on the plantation for six years. His education began at St. Mary's Seminary and University in Maryland, then Jesuit College in New Orleans, and finally Georgetown University in Washington, D.C. At sixteen Edward left school to join the Confederate army. He served and was captured by Federal troops at the Battle of Port Hudson, but was paroled soon after his capture, as were many of the other Confederate prisoners from that battle.

After the Civil War, Edward Douglass White II returned to school to study law. He passed the bar at age twenty-three and was one of the attorneys involved in establishing Tulane University. In 1874 White was elected to the state senate, becoming active in the movement to overthrow the repressive "carpet bagger" rule during the Reconstruction. As a legislator he also fought the scandalous Louisiana lottery and became a proponent of improved Mississippi River levee construction.

In 1879 Edward Douglass White II became an associate justice of the Louisiana Supreme Court. He later became a U.S. senator, and in 1891 President Grover Cleveland appointed him as an associate justice of the U.S. Supreme Court. In 1910 he became chief justice by decree of President Howard Taft, the only native Louisianian to reach the position on the Supreme Court. A statue of Chief Justice White stands in front of the Louisiana court building in New Orleans.

The house and park are located on Louisiana Highway 1, approximately five miles north of Thibodaux, along Bayou Lafourche. A small admission is charged to view the house, which contains original furnishings, artifacts, and pictures, including one of Robert E. Lee, autographed by the general himself.

References

Arrigo, Joseph A., and Cara M. Batt. *Plantations*. Stillwater, MN: Voyageur Press, 1989.

Bannon, Lois Elmer. *Magnolia Mound: A Louisiana River Plantation*. Gretna, LA: Pelican, 1984.

Butler, W. E. *Down Among the Sugar Cane*. Baton Rouge, LA: Claitors, 1980.

Calhoun, James, and Susan Dore. *Louisiana Almanac 1988–89*. Gretna, LA: Pelican, 1988.

Casso, Evans J. *Louisiana Legacy: History of the National Guard*, Gretna, LA: Pelican, 1976.

Conrad, Glenn R. *St. Charles, Abstracts of the Civil Records, 1700–1803*. Lafayette, LA: Center for Louisiana Studies, 1974.

Cooper, F. Wesley. *Louisiana*. Natchez, MS: Wesley, 1961.

Eakin, Sue. *Rapides Parish, An Illustrated History*. Northridge, CA: Windsor, 1987.

Gleason, David King. *Plantations of Louisiana and Natchez*. Baton Rouge, LA: Louisiana State University Press, 1983.

Kane, Harnett. *Plantation Parade*. New York: Bonanza, 1945.

Laughlin, Clarence John. *Ghosts Along the Mississippi: The Magic of Old Houses of Louisiana*. New York: Crown, 1981.

Malone, Paul. *Louisiana Plantation Homes, A Return to Splendor*. Gretna, LA: Pelican, 1986.

Malone, Lee. *The Majesty of the River Road*. Gretna, LA: Pelican, 1988.

Overdyke, W. Darrell. *Louisiana Plantation Homes*. New York: Outlet, 1965.

Pelican Guide to Plantation Homes of Louisiana, 7th Ed. Gretna, LA: Pelican, 1988.

Reeves, Miriam G. *The Felicianas of Louisiana*. Baton Rouge, LA: Claitors, 1967.

Seebold, Herman deBachelle. *Old Louisiana Plantation Homes and Family Trees, Vols. I & II*. New Orleans, LA: Seebold, 1941.

Smith, J. Fraser. *White Pillars*. New York: Bramhall House, 1941.

Stahls, Paul F. Jr. *Plantation Homes of the Lafourche Country*. Gretna, LA: Pelican, 1976.

Stahls, Paul F. Jr. *Plantation Homes of the Teche Country*. Gretna, LA: Pelican, 1979.

Stuart, Josepha, and Wilson Gathings. *Great Southern Mansions*. New York: Walker and Co., 1977.

Vals-Denuzier, Jacqueline P. *Homes of the Planters*. Baton Rouge, LA: Claitors, 1984.